THIS NOTEBOOK BELONGS TO

CONTACT

Do you Feather?

See our range of fine, illustrated books, ebooks, notebooks and art calendars:
www.flametreepublishing.com

This is a **FLAME TREE NOTEBOOK**
Published and © copyright 2016 Flame Tree Publishing Ltd

FTPB27 • ISBN 978-1-78664-068-0

Cover image based on
Moon Maiden by Jean and Ron Henry
All works courtesy of the artists, © Jean and Ron Henry 1985-2014,
© Peter Henry 2015-2017

FLAME TREE PUBLISHING | The Art of Fine Gifts
6 Melbray Mews, London SW6 3NS, United Kingdom